THE SEARCH FOR
ANTARCTIC DINOSAURS

By
Sally M. Walker

Illustrated by
John Bindon

On My Own
SCIENCE

M Millbrook Press/Minneapolis

Note to readers: Say the word *Cryolophosaurus ellioti* like cry-oh-LOHF-oh-SOHR-uhs eh-lee-AH-tee.

The author and artist would like to thank Dr. William Hammer and Susan Kornreich Wolf of the Fryxell Geology Museum, Augustana College, for patiently answering our many questions, reading the manuscript for accuracy, and providing an invaluable assortment of visual reference that helped bring this book to life.

Millbrook Press, Inc.
A division of Lerner Publishing Group, Inc.
241 First Avenue North
Minneapolis, MN 55401 U.S.A.

Website address: www.lernerbooks.com

Library of Congress Cataloging-in-Publication Data

Walker, Sally M.
    The search for Antarctic dinosaurs / by Sally M. Walker ; illustrations by John Bindon.
       p.   cm. — (On my own science)
    Includes bibliographical references.
    ISBN-13: 978–0–8225–6749–3 (lib. bdg. : alk. paper)
    1. Dinosaurs—Antarctica—Juvenile literature. 2. Fossils—Antarctica—Juvenile literature. I. Bindon, John, ill. II. Title.
    QE861.5.W34 2008
    567.909989—dc22   2006028779

Manufactured in the United States of America
1 2 3 4 5 6 – JR – 13 12 11 10 09 08

To Jameson Rush—There are a gazillion fossils
waiting to be discovered. May your fondest paleontological
dreams come true. Just remember: Always dream BIG!
—SMW

To my mother and late father,
who have always supported my career choice and showed
interest in any project I was involved with
—JB

An Antarctic Surprise

January 1991

Rocks, ice, and snow.

At first, that was all

Dr. William Hammer and his crew saw

when they looked at the land around them.

No plants grow in the area.

No animals live there either.

It's just too cold.

Dr. Hammer is a paleontologist.
Paleontologists are scientists
who study fossils.
Fossils are the hardened remains
of plants and animals.
After an animal or plant dies,
soil and sand may cover it.

Over thousands of years,
the remains of the plant or animal
may turn to stone.
Then they are called fossils.
Bones, shells, stems, leaves,
and even footprints can become fossils.

North America

Europe

Asia

Africa

South America

Australia

Antarctica

Dr. Hammer and his students
search for fossils in Antarctica.
Antarctica is a continent.
Continents are Earth's large land areas.
Antarctica is Earth's coldest continent.
Ice and snow cover much of its surface.
In the winter, only tall mountain peaks
rise above the thick ice.

Most of the year,
Antarctica is too cold
for fossil hunting.
Hammer and his crew can
search only in the summer.
Summer in Antarctica
lasts from December
to January.
Then the sun shines
almost 24 hours a day.
Even so, the air temperature
where Hammer works
is usually –25 to –30 degrees
Fahrenheit.
And some areas can get
very windy.
Wind makes the air
feel even colder.

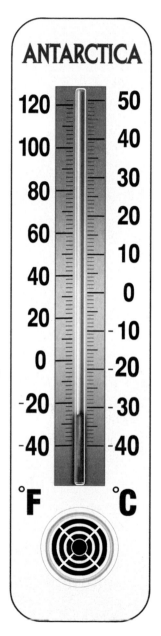

0°

to Africa

Atlantic Ocean

James Ross Island
Vega Island
Seymour Island

to South America

ANTARCTICA

90°W ——————— ■ **South Pole** ——————— 90°E

• **Mount Kirkpatrick**

■ **McMurdo Station**

Ross Island

Pacific Ocean

to Australia

to New Zealand

MAP KEY
• fossil site
■ research station

180°

This was not Hammer's first trip
to Antarctica.
On earlier visits, he had found many fossils.
He found fossil bones and teeth.
They belonged to reptiles that had lived
more than 200 million years ago.
Dinosaurs lived then too.
Fossil hunters had found dinosaur fossils
on islands near Antarctica.
But no one had ever found a dinosaur fossil
on the main part of Antarctica.

On this trip,

Hammer had received a radio message.

It was from David Elliot,

a scientist who was studying rocks nearby.

Elliot thought some of the rocks

looked as if they had bones in them.

Hammer went to see the rocks.

What he saw thrilled him.

Elliot was right.

The rocks did have bones in them!

Hammer knew that the rock surrounding

the bones was very old.

It had formed about 190 million years ago.

Could some of these bones

be dinosaur bones?

Hammer decided to find out.

He would come back with a team

to study these bones.

Fossil Hunting in Antarctica

Searching for fossils in Antarctica
is a big project.
It takes a lot of planning.
Hammer and his crew had to fly
from the United States
to a country called New Zealand.
There, they were outfitted with clothes
for their expedition.

15

Every scientist needed long underwear
and fleece shirts.

The crew chose warm pants.

They also got thin, windproof pants.

They wore these pants
over their regular pants.

They also needed two jackets.

One was a lightweight jacket.

The other was a thick one.

The scientists got special boots too.

The boots had a layer of air inside them.

The air helped keep their feet warm.

The soles of the boots were rough.

They could grip slippery surfaces
or jagged rocks.

The crew also needed hats and gloves.

Sunglasses and sunblock
protected their eyes and skin from the sun.

After they received their special clothing,
the scientists flew to Antarctica.
Their first stop was McMurdo Station
on Ross Island.
Ross Island is just off the coast
of Antarctica.
At McMurdo, Hammer and his crew
received more supplies.

They got tents and sleeping bags.
They got cookstoves and food.
There are no stores in the area
where they would be working.
The crew had to make sure
they had enough food
to last two months.

Before Hammer and his crew left McMurdo,
they also went to a training school.
For several days, the crew took lessons.
They learned how to work in cold places.
If the scientists weren't careful,
parts of their skin and body
could freeze.

The crew knew they'd be on mountains
while they hunted for fossils.
On the tops of tall mountains,
there is less oxygen in the air.
Oxygen is the gas we breathe to stay alive.
The scientists learned to move and breathe
in ways that would help them
get enough oxygen.
They also learned how to climb rocky cliffs
and cross dangerous ice.
Antarctic ice has deep cracks.
People have been killed falling into them.
The crew learned how to travel safely on ice.
After Hammer's crew learned these skills,
they were ready to hunt for fossils!

Getting the Bones

A plane with skis for landing
flew Hammer and his crew inland.
After the plane landed on the ice,
the scientists set up a base camp.
A base camp is where the crew eats,
sleeps, and stores supplies.
It would be their home
for three to ten weeks.

Base camp was about 5,000 feet higher
than the land around McMurdo.
But that's not where David Elliot
saw the bones.
That spot was about 40 miles
from base camp on Mount Kirkpatrick.
Mount Kirkpatrick is about 15,000 feet high!
The only way Hammer could reach the site
was by helicopter.

Each day, a helicopter flew Hammer and
his crew from base camp to
where the fossils were.
Sometimes, strong winds or snowstorms
made it too dangerous to fly.
The crew had to wait at base camp
until the weather improved.

Getting to the site was only half
the problem.
Collecting the fossils was the other half.
The fossils Elliot found
were still inside a rocky cliff.
How could Hammer remove the fossils
from the rock?

Hammer's crew used a jackhammer
to remove chucks of rock from the cliff.
They did not use the jackhammer
in places where it would damage a fossil.
Instead, they used rock hammers
to break away small bits of rock.
Hammer grew more excited as he
carefully studied the edges
of bones he could see.
The fossil bones looked as if they belonged
to a big animal.
Could the crew find the animal's
complete skeleton?
They had to remove more rock to find out.

Over the next three weeks,
the scientists traveled back and forth
from their base camp to Mount Kirkpatrick.
They struggled against the wind and cold.
Piece by piece, Hammer's crew
removed 5,000 pounds of rock
that contained fossils.
The helicopter carried the rock
to base camp.

Hammer further examined the fossils there.

He could see part of a big skull.

He saw ribs and leg bones.

There were bones from the back and tail.

What Hammer saw

certainly looked like a dinosaur—

maybe even more than one.

But rock still surrounded the bones.

Hammer couldn't see enough of each bone
to figure out what kind of animal
the crew had found.
He had to take the chunks of rock
to his laboratory in the United States.
There he had special tools
for removing fossils from rocks.

The crew carefully packed the fossil-filled
rocks so they wouldn't break.
The ski plane flew the boxes to Ross Island.
Then they were put onto a big ship.
Hammer didn't see them again
until months later.
By then, he was very eager to find out
exactly what his crew had collected.

The dinosaur had large, pointed teeth.

That meant it was a meat eater.

It had an odd-looking bony ridge

on its head.

The ridge is called a crest.

Clearly, the crew had found a new dinosaur.

That meant Hammer could name it.

He named the dinosaur

Cryolophosaurus ellioti.

Cryolophosaurus means

"frozen crested lizard."

Ellioti comes from David Elliot's last name.

Hammer wanted to name the dinosaur after

the scientist who told him about the bones.

During later expeditions to Antarctica,

Hammer returned to the same fossil site.

Each time, his crew found more bones

that belonged to *Cryolophosaurus ellioti.*

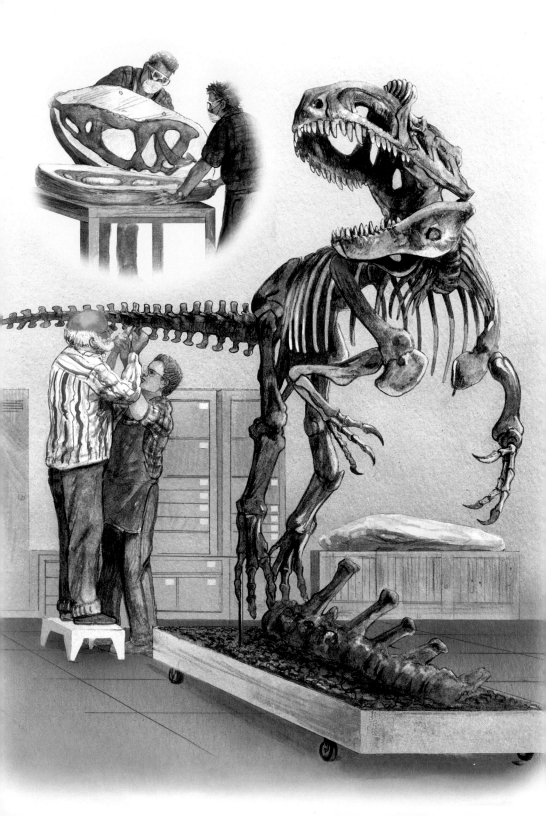

In the U.S. laboratory, the paleontologists
made molds of the bones they found.
They used the molds
to make plastic copies of the bones.
They also made models of bones
that were missing.
They made the models look like the bones
found in similar dinosaurs.
The plastic "bones" and models
were put together.
They formed a complete
Cryolophosaurus skeleton.
Hammer learned a lot from the bones.
Cryolophosaurus was about 22 feet long.
Its skull was almost 2 feet long.
And it walked upright on two legs,
like the dinosaur called *Allosaurus*.

More Exciting News

Cryolophosaurus wasn't the only fossil
Hammer's crew found.
There was a wing bone from a
small pterosaur.
Pterosaurs were flying reptiles.
They lived at the same time as dinosaurs.

The paleontologists measured
the pterosaur bone.
They think the pterosaur's wings
may have spread as wide as 3 to 6 feet.
That's about 1 foot smaller
than the wingspan of a bald eagle.

The crew also discovered fossil teeth
from at least two other dinosaurs.
They found the teeth
with the bones of *Cryolophosaurus*.
Some of its bones had tooth marks on them.
Hammer thinks that after
Cryolophosaurus died,
other meat-eating dinosaurs ate its body.
Their teeth may have broken off
while eating.
But how did *Cryolophosaurus* die?

Hammer thinks he knows the answer
to that too.
When his assistant cleaned
the *Cryolophosaurus* skull,
he made an exciting discovery.
There were two rib bones
inside the jaws of *Cryolophosaurus*.
The ribs were far back in its mouth.
They belonged to a large
plant-eating dinosaur.
Hammer thinks *Cryolophosaurus*
may have choked to death while eating it!

The rocks and fossils Hammer collected
have told him a lot about the fossil site.
The rock containing the fossils
was originally mud.
It was the kind of mud
that is found near rivers.
Near the fossil site, Hammer's team
had found fossilized trees.
That meant *Cryolophosaurus* had lived
and died on land near a river and forests.
But it's too cold in that part of Antarctica
for modern-day plants to grow.
And dinosaurs could not live in
very cold places.
What did this information tell Hammer?
It told him that when
dinosaurs roamed the land,
Antarctica must have been much warmer.

In December 2003 to January 2004,
Dr. Hammer's crew made another
exciting Antarctic discovery.
They found bones that belonged to
a 200-million-year-old dinosaur.
Hammer thinks it is a completely new kind
of plant-eating dinosaur.
But they don't know much about it yet.
The rest of its bones still lie hidden inside
Antarctica's rocks.
Perhaps the fossils of many more dinosaurs
remain buried in the rocks.
Dr. Hammer and future paleontologists
must return to Antarctica
to learn the fossils' stories.

Afterword

William Hammer's discovery of *Cryolophosaurus* has added an exciting chapter to Antarctic life. But the dinosaur fossils found in other areas of Antarctica are fascinating too. Vega, Seymour, and James Ross islands are all located near the base of Antarctica's fingerlike peninsula. They are treasure troves of dinosaur fossils. Because these islands have little plant life or ice, the fossils are easier to locate and collect. Paleontologists have found fossils from a duck-billed dinosaur and an iguanodon-like dinosaur on the rocky shores of the islands.

Other fascinating Antarctic fossils found on these islands include bones from two kinds of large ocean reptiles named mosasaurs and plesiosaurs, flat shells from organisms that looked like oysters, curled-up shells made by creatures called ammonites, and bones from fishes. Future expeditions to different areas of Antarctica will likely add more intriguing pieces to the puzzle of Antarctica's past.

Glossary

base camp: the place where a group of people eats, sleeps, and stores supplies for a time

continent (KAHN-tuh-nuhnt): one of Earth's very large land areas. North America, South America, Europe, Asia, Africa, Australia, and Antarctica are continents.

crest: a hollow, bony ridge on a dinosaur's head

expedition (EHK-spuh-DIH-shuhn): a long trip taken for a special purpose, such as to explore an area

fossils (FAH-suhlz): the hardened remains, tracks, or traces of something that lived long ago

paleontologist (PAY-lee-uhn-TAH-luh-jihst): a scientist who studies fossils

pterosaur (TEHR-uh-sawr): a member of a group of flying reptiles that lived before and during the time of dinosaurs

reptiles (REHP-tylz): crawling or creeping animals that have scales

site: the place where something is located

Further Reading and Websites

Antarctic Photo Library
  http://photolibrary.usap.gov/
Bears on Ice 2005
  http://www.ku-prism.org/resources/Bears2005/
Chrisp, Peter. *Dinosaur Detectives*. New York: Dorling Kindersley, 2001.
DinoLand Travels Database: Fryxell Geology Museum-Augustana College
  http://www.geocities.com/stegob/augustana.html
Discovering Antarctica—Teaching and Learning Resources on Antarctica
  http://www.discoveringantarctica.org.uk/index.php
Goodman, Susan E. *Life on the Ice*. Minneapolis: Millbrook Press, 2006.
Hooper, Meredith. *The Island That Moved: How Shifting Forces Shape Our Earth*. New York: Viking, 2004.
Walker, Sally M. *Fossils*. Minneapolis: Lerner Publications Company, 2007.
ZOOM SCHOOL Antarctica by EnchantedLearning.com
  http://www.enchantedlearning.com/school/Antarctica/

Selected Bibliography

Discover Magazine. "The Frozen Crested Lizard." September 1994.
Hammer, William R. Interview by Sally M. Walker. Augustana College, Rock Island, Illinois. December 2005.
Hammer, William R., James W. Collinson, and William J. Ryan III. "A New Triassic Vertebrate Fauna from Antarctica and Its Depositional Setting." *Antarctica Science* 2, no. 2 (1990): 163–167.
Hammer, William R., and William J. Hickerson. "A Crested Theropod Dinosaur from Antarctica." *Science* 264, no. 5160 (1994): 828–830.
Mullen, William. "Breaking New Dino Ground." *Chicago Tribune*, January 25, 2004, Metro section.
National Geographic. "Antarctic Peak Yields a Dinosaur Drama." October 1994, Geographica section.